AF483204

Dedication

To my grandma, the best friend
in the universe.

A portion of book sales will be donated to
Love For Our Elders
(loveforourelders.org),
a nonprofit I started to fight loneliness
one letter at a time.

Library of Congress Control Number: 2022911752

ISBN: 979-8-218-26147-4

Illustrated and designed by Angelika Scudamore

Published in Cleveland, Ohio. Printed in the United States of America.

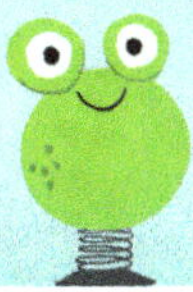

Grandma's Letter Exchange

Jacob Cramer

Angelika Scudamore

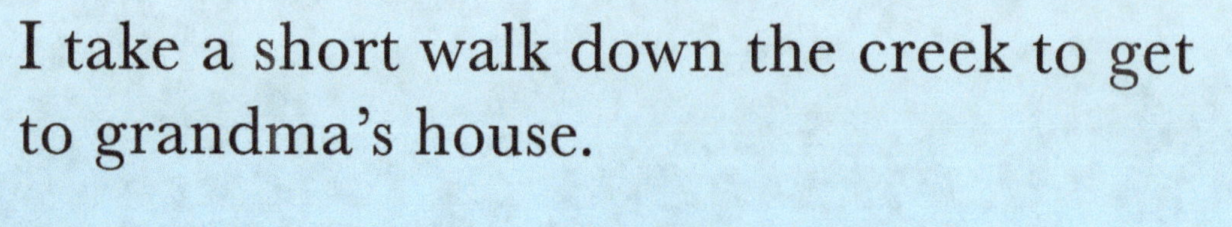

I take a short walk down the creek to get
to grandma's house.

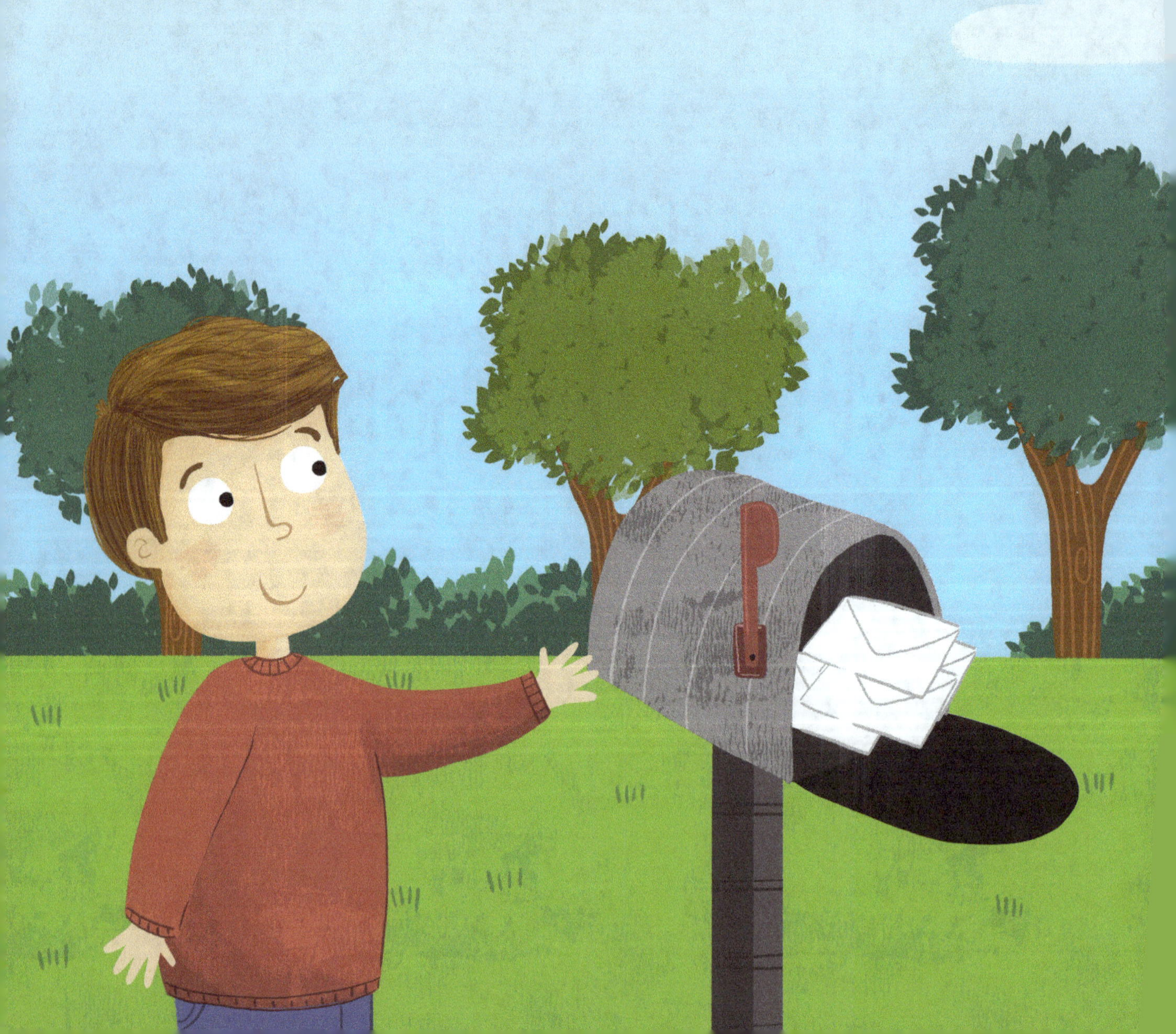

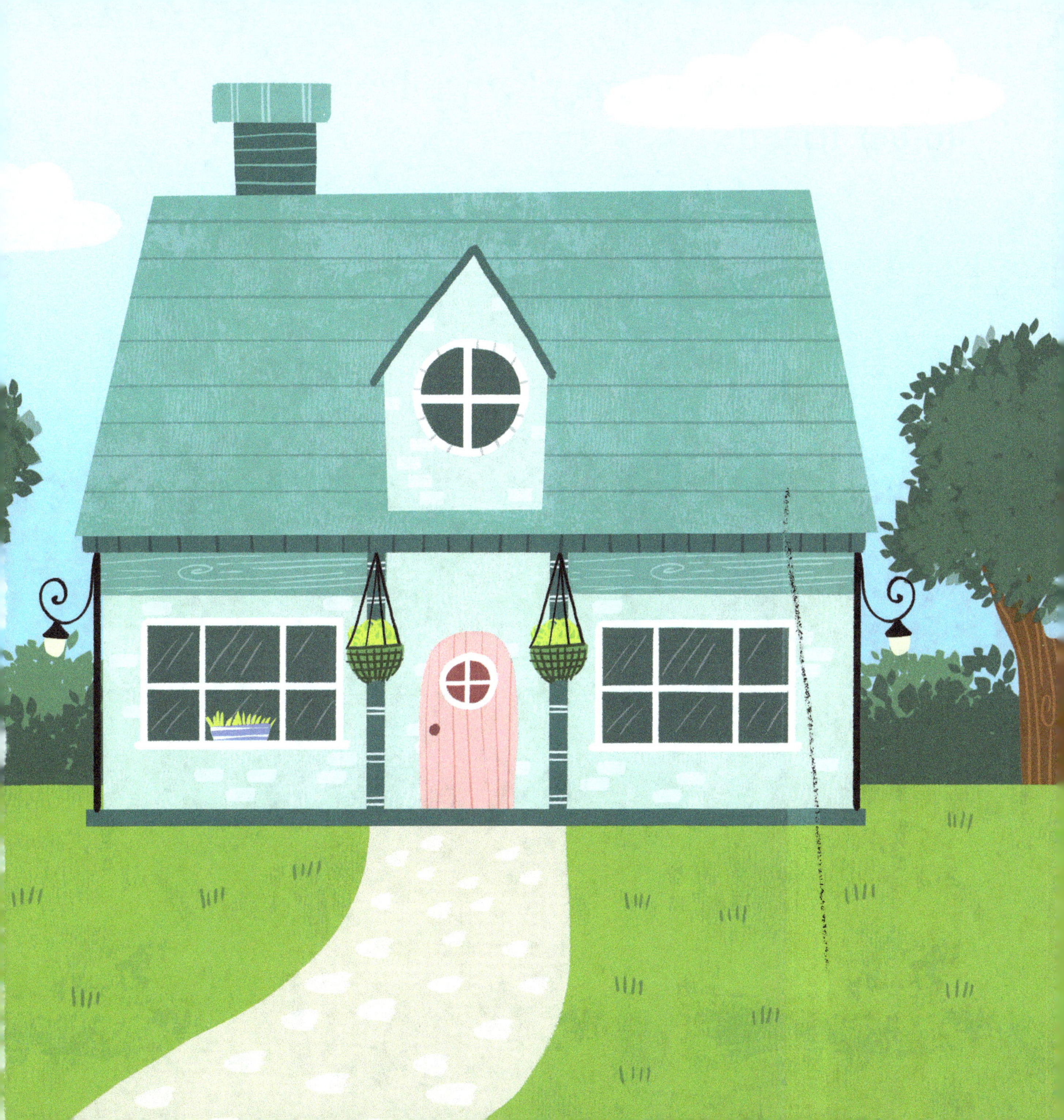

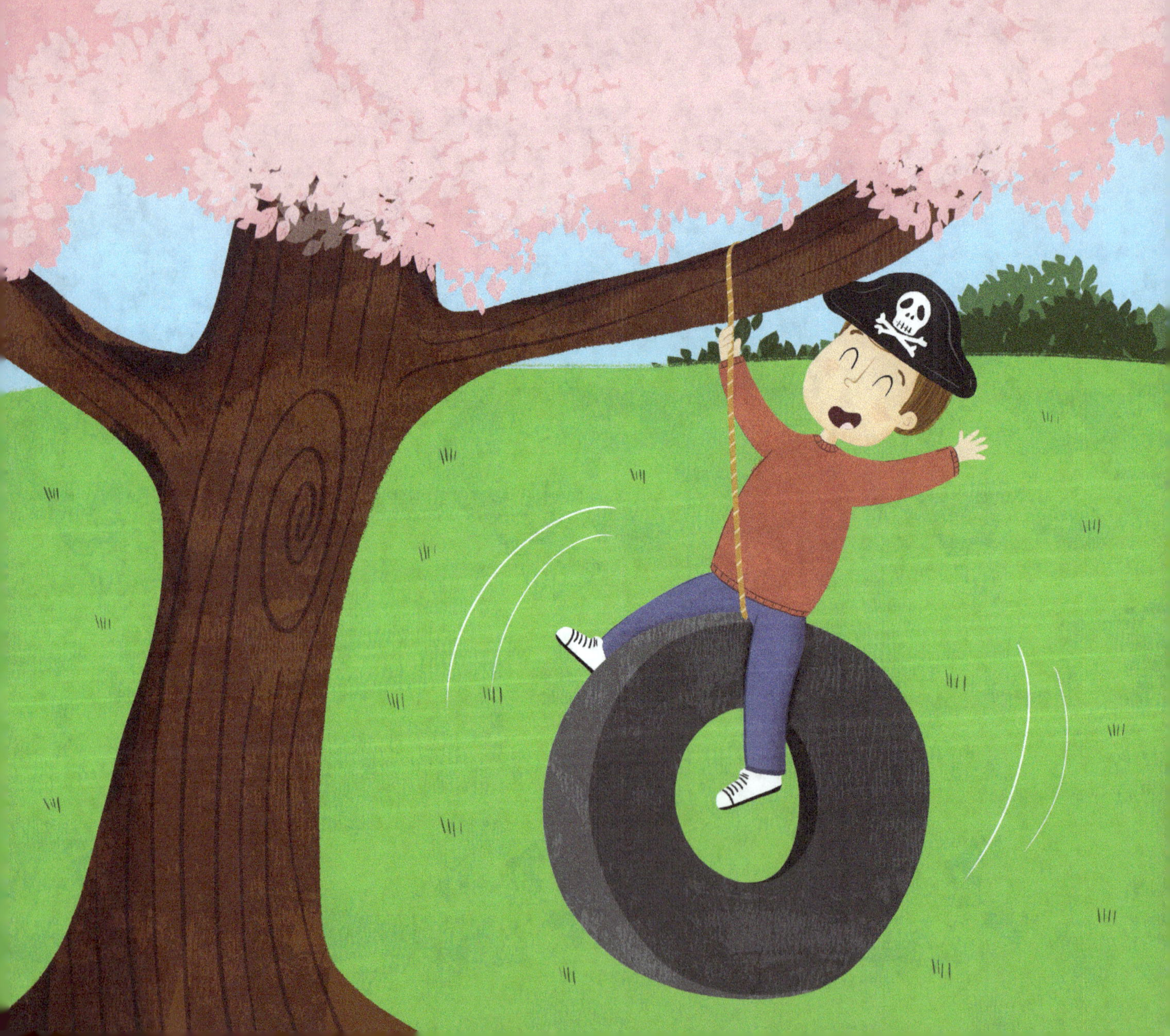

Grandma watches me play while she writes letters to her friends.

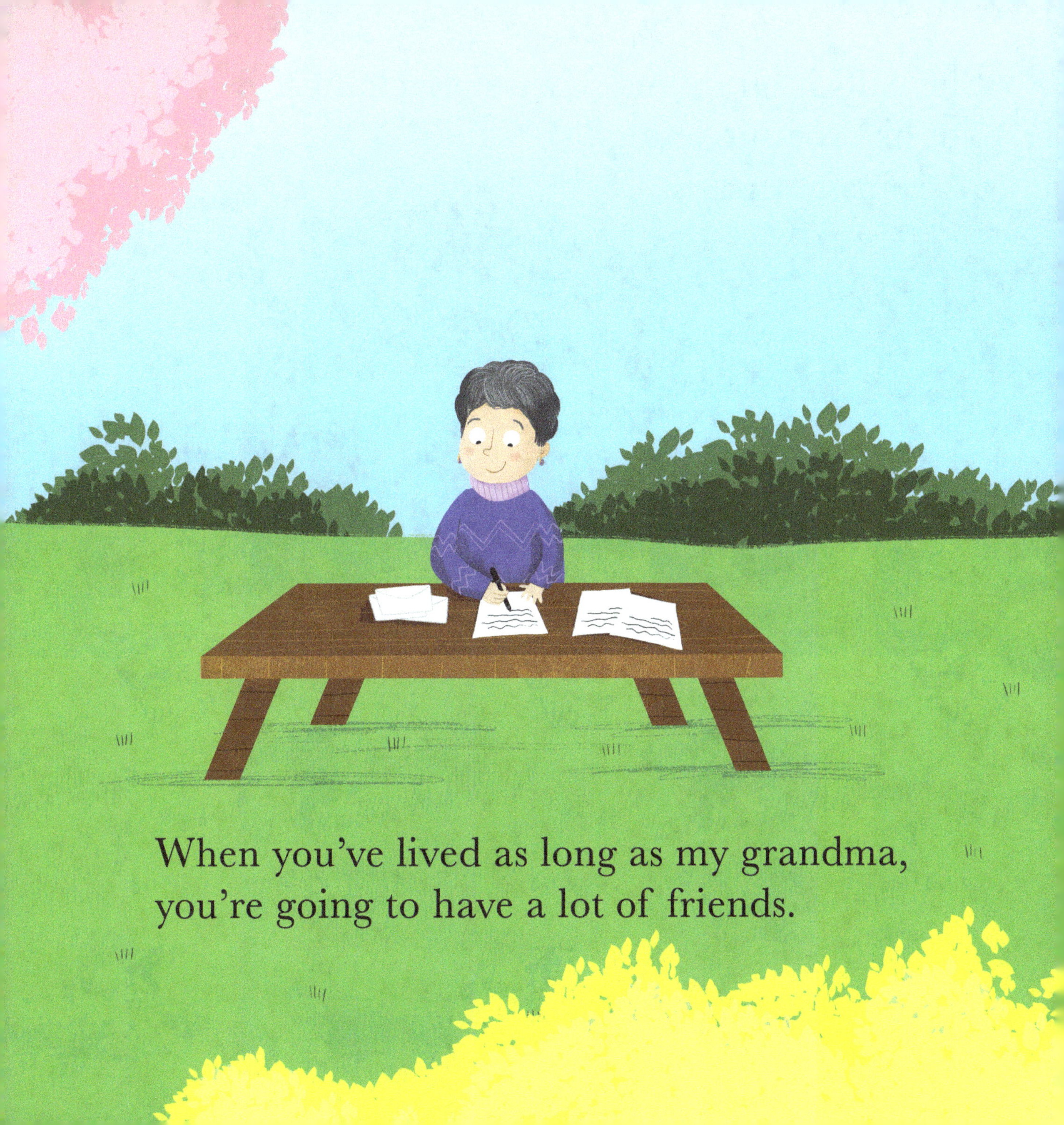

When you've lived as long as my grandma,
you're going to have a lot of friends.

She calls it Grandma's Letter Exchange. But I do
not like writing letters.
It seems boring.

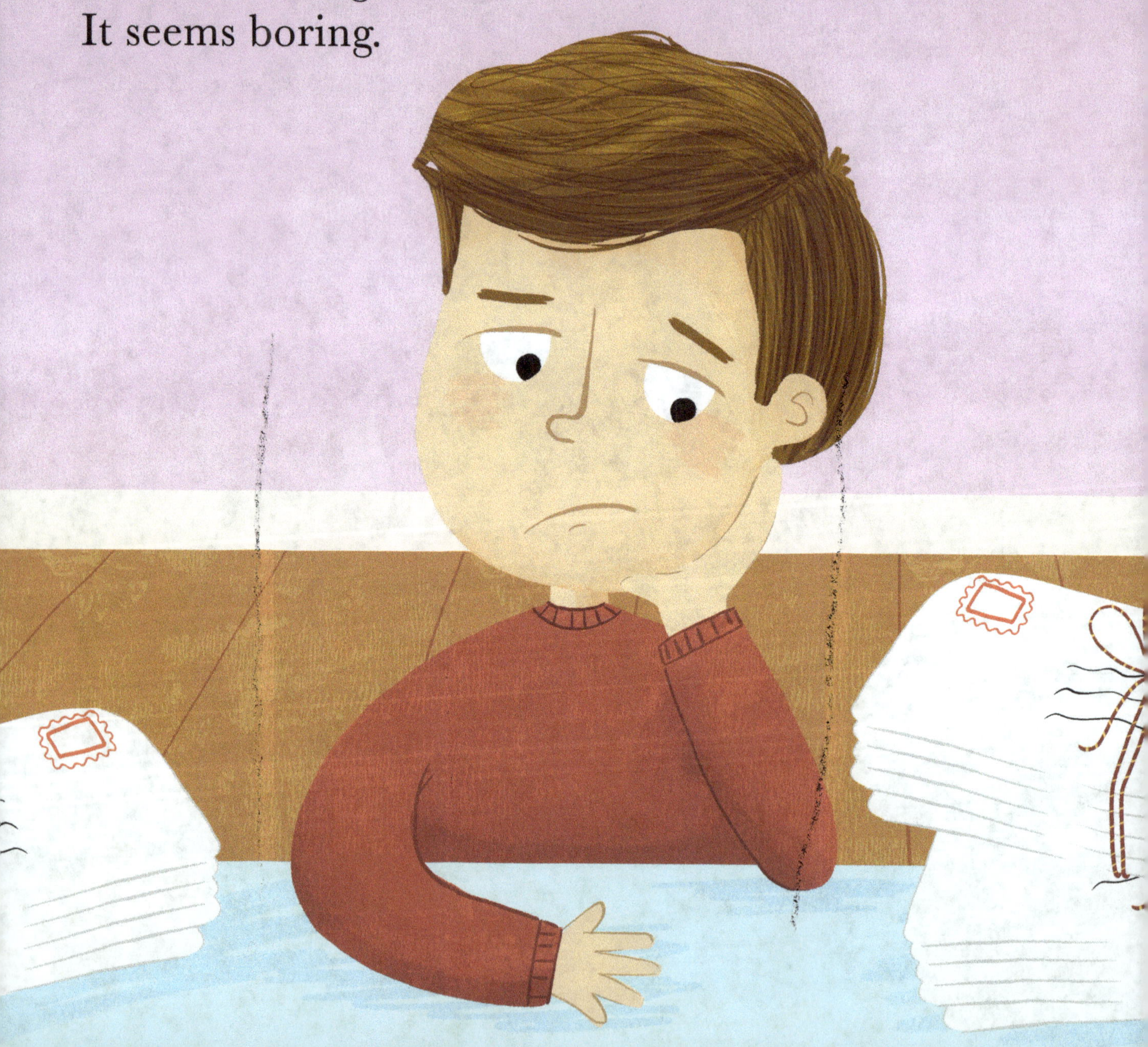

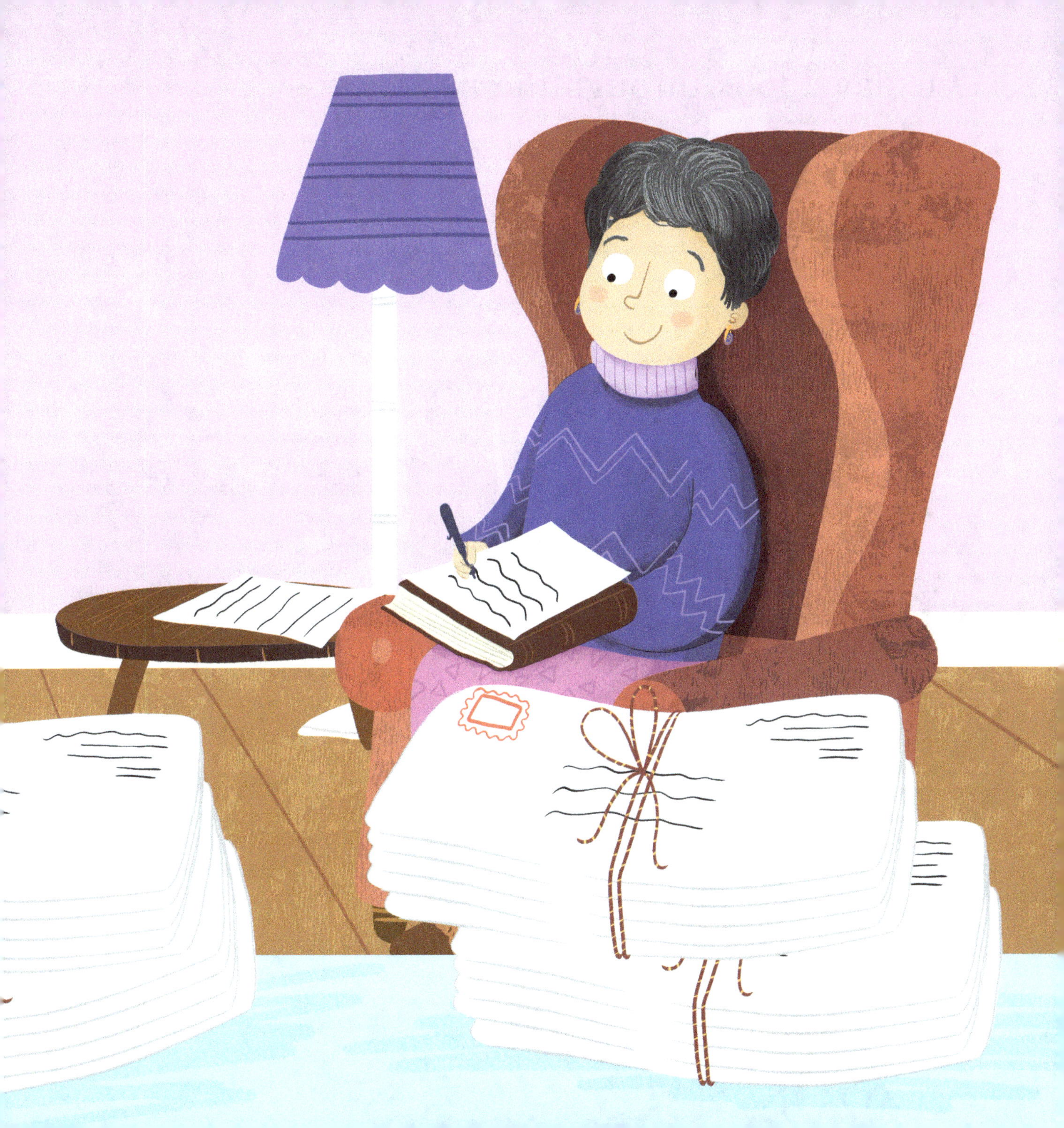

One day, I look through the
window and she's not in
her usual chair.

I search everywhere…

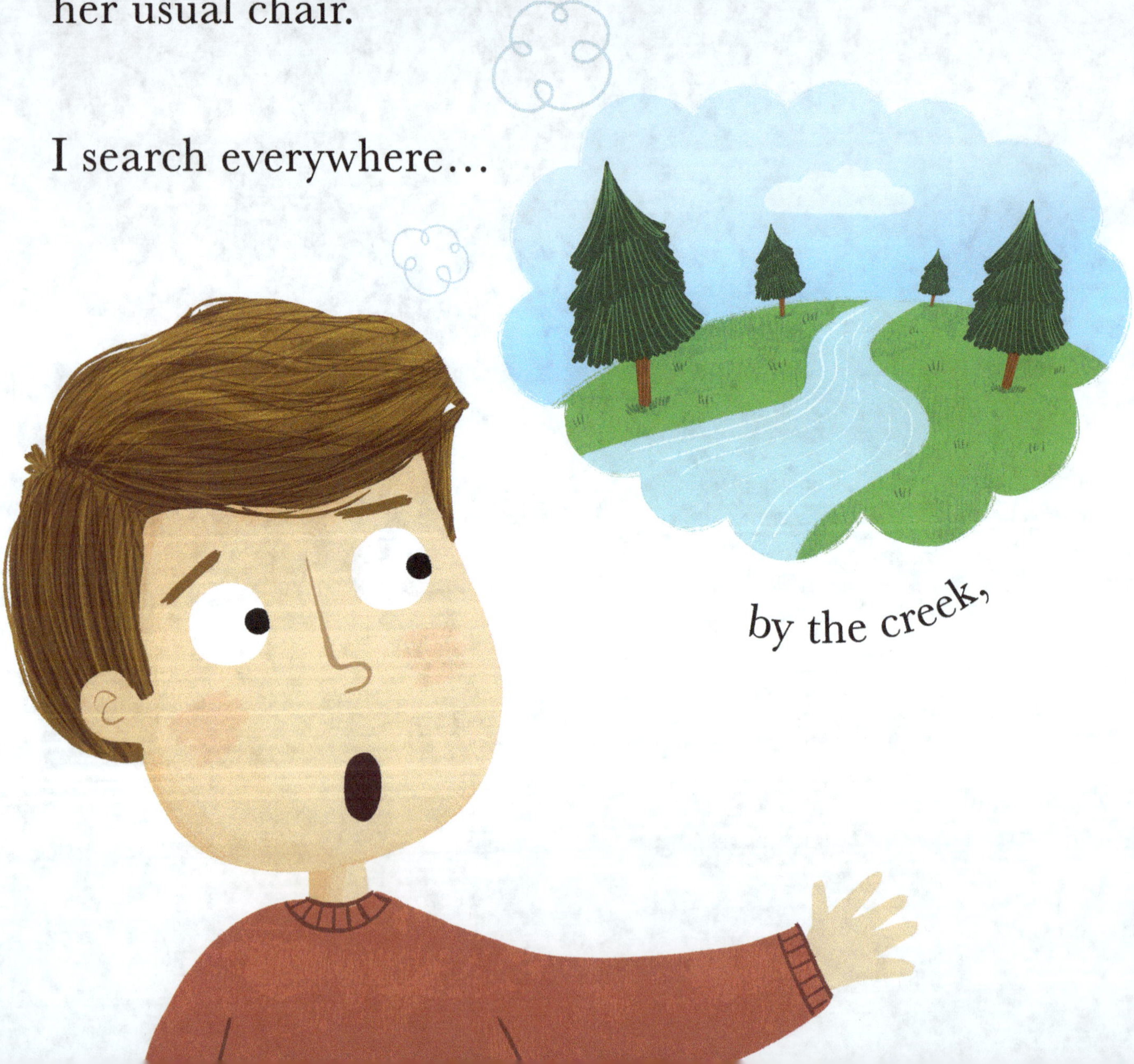

by the creek,

in the garden,

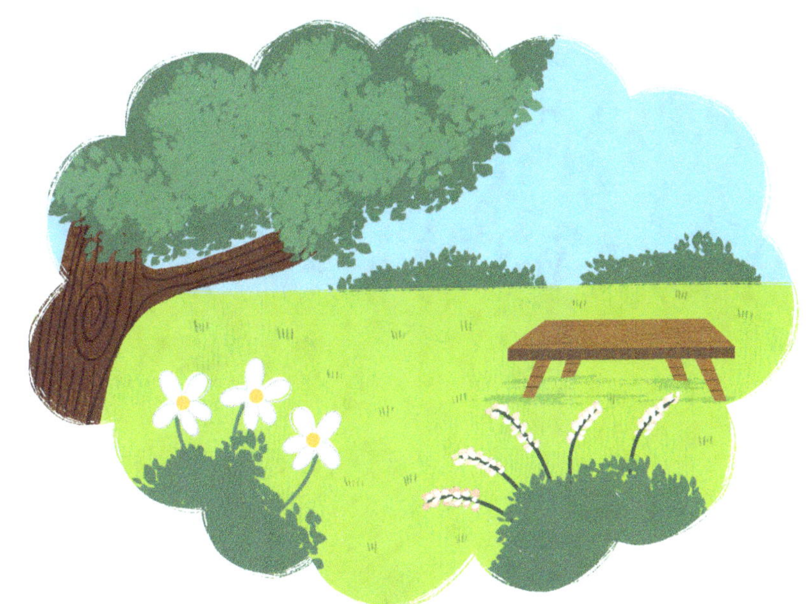

and even through the trees.

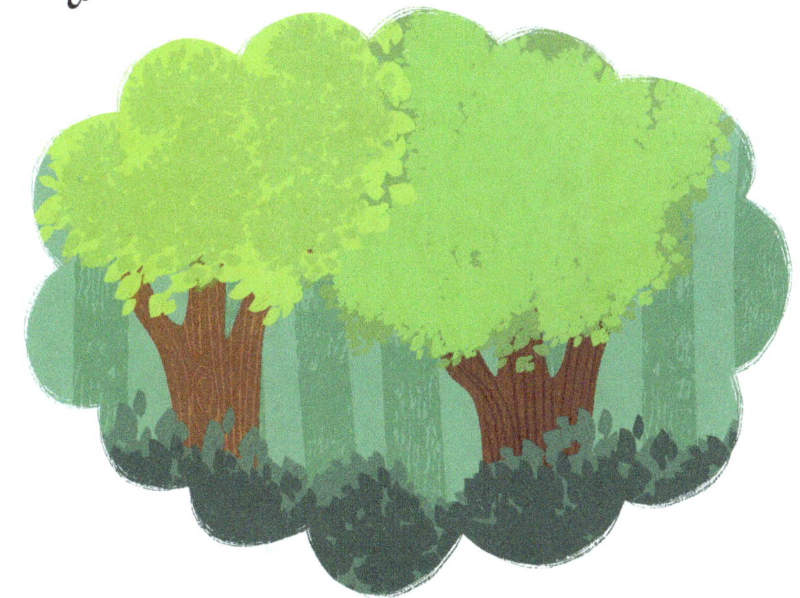

I don't see her
anywhere.

She's probably
mailing her letters.

Just as I'm about to leave, I hear grandma shout from the porch,

"Hey you! Want to see something new?"

"Grandma, a rocket! Can we go in?" I ask.

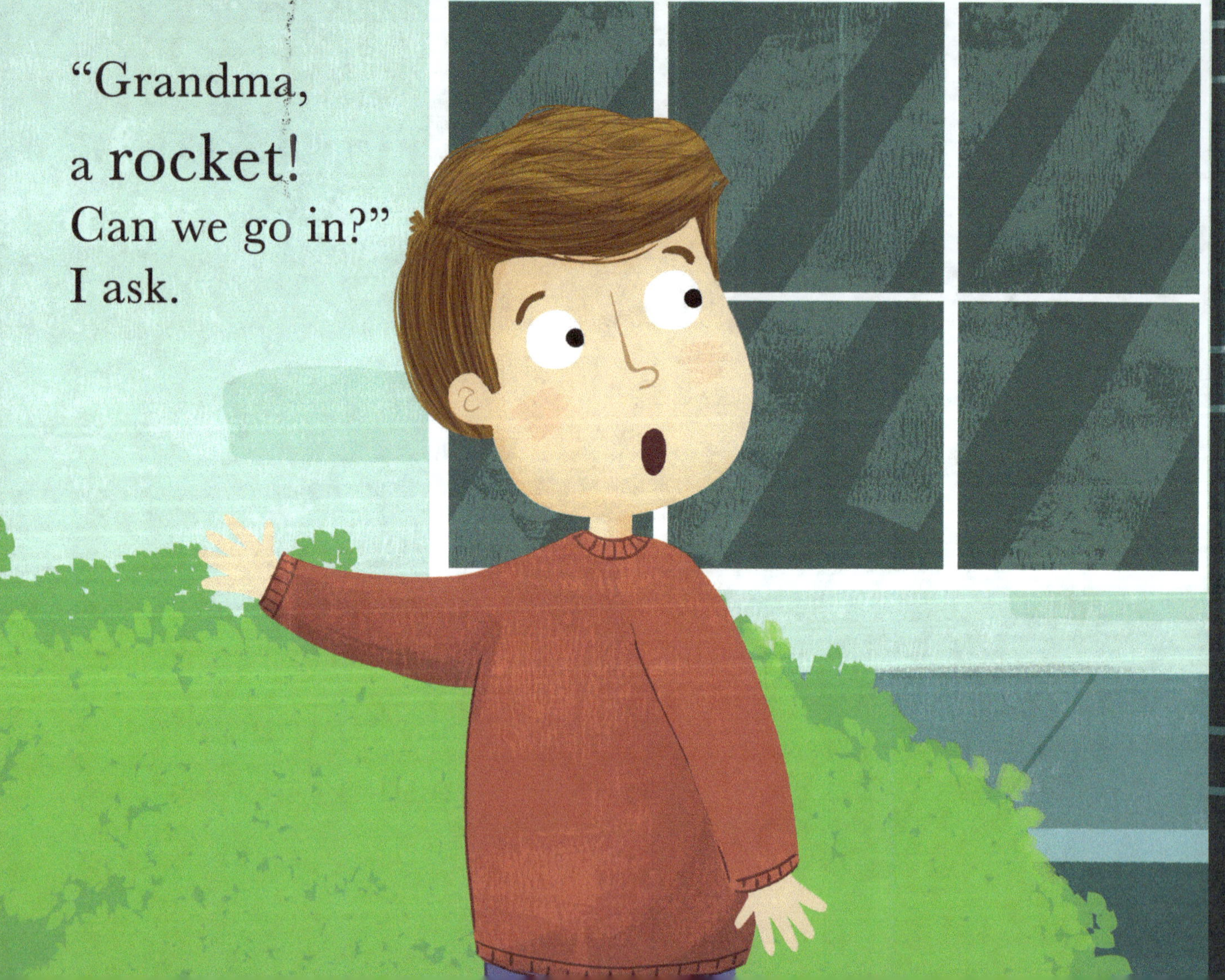

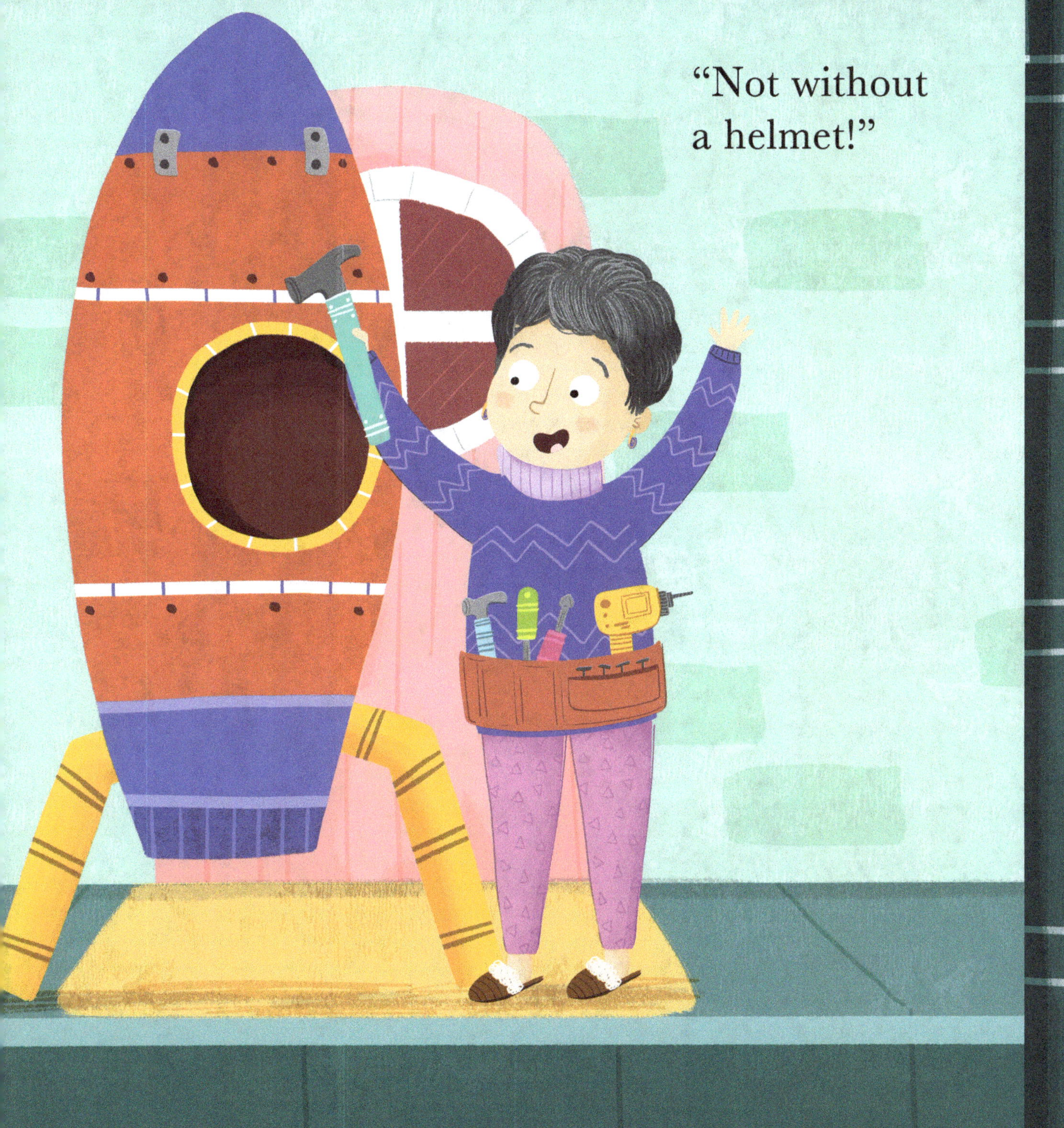

"Not without
a helmet!"

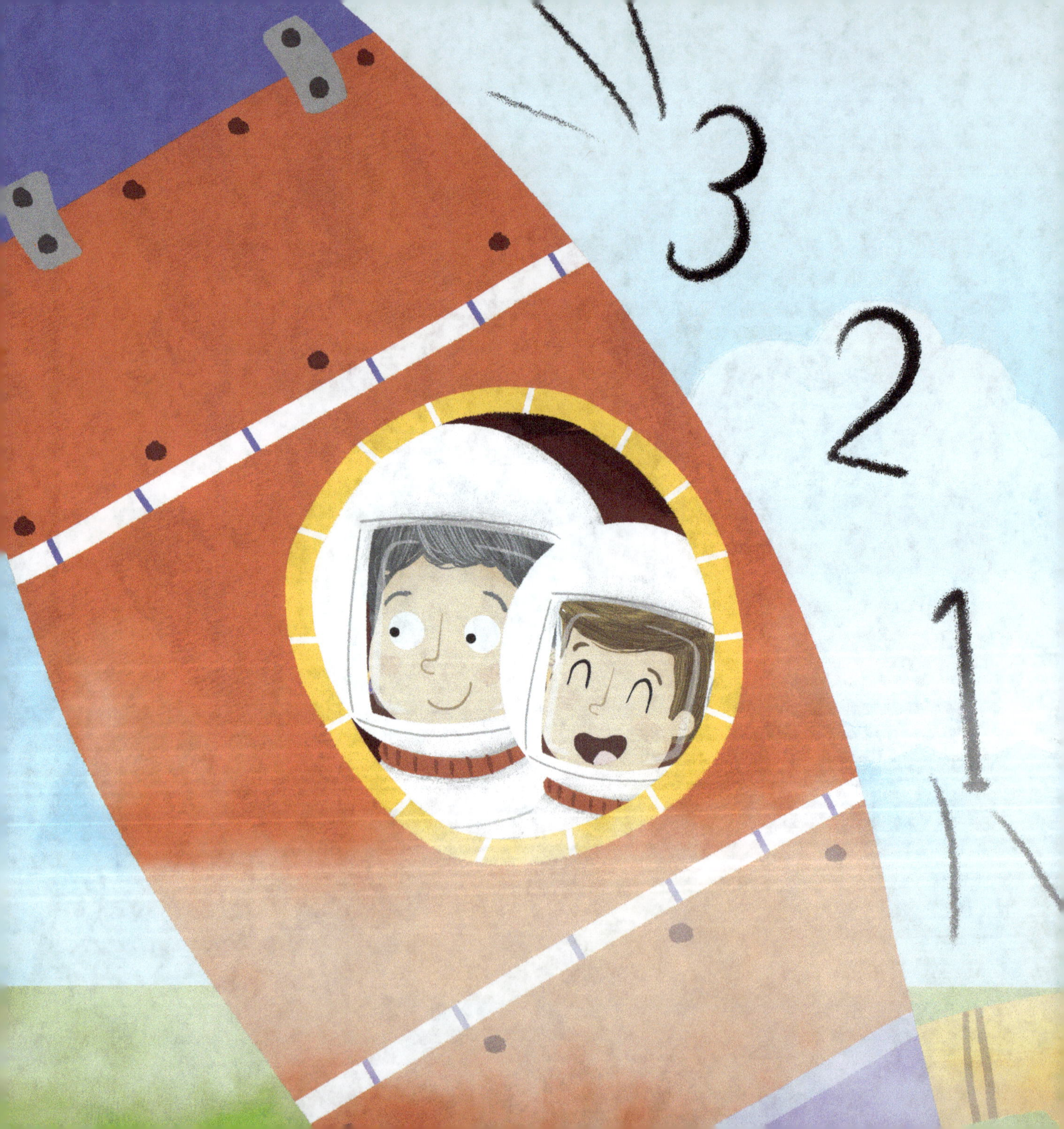

3
2
1

We count down together. "3, 2, 1...
Blast off!"

Soon, Grandma's house becomes very small.

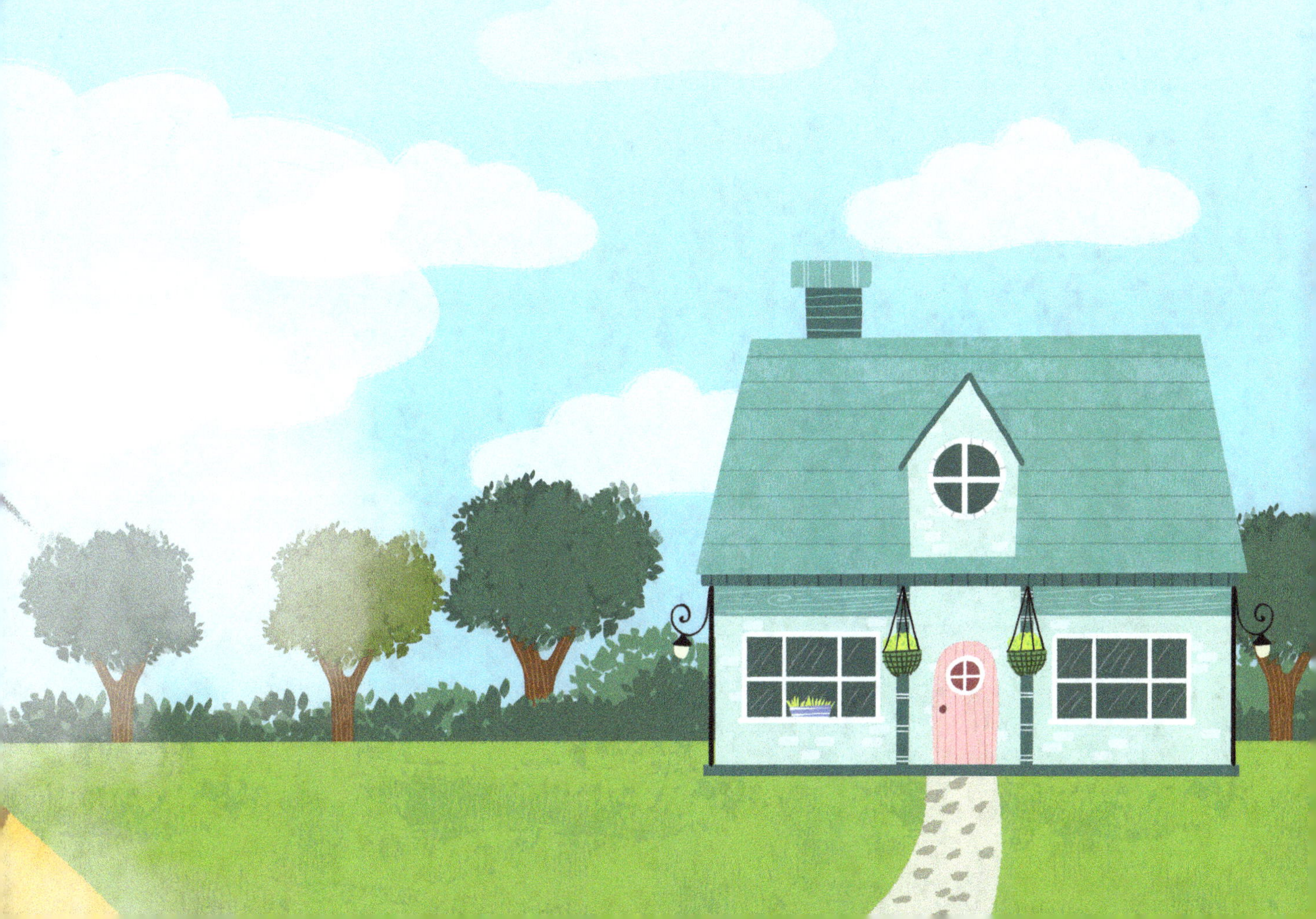

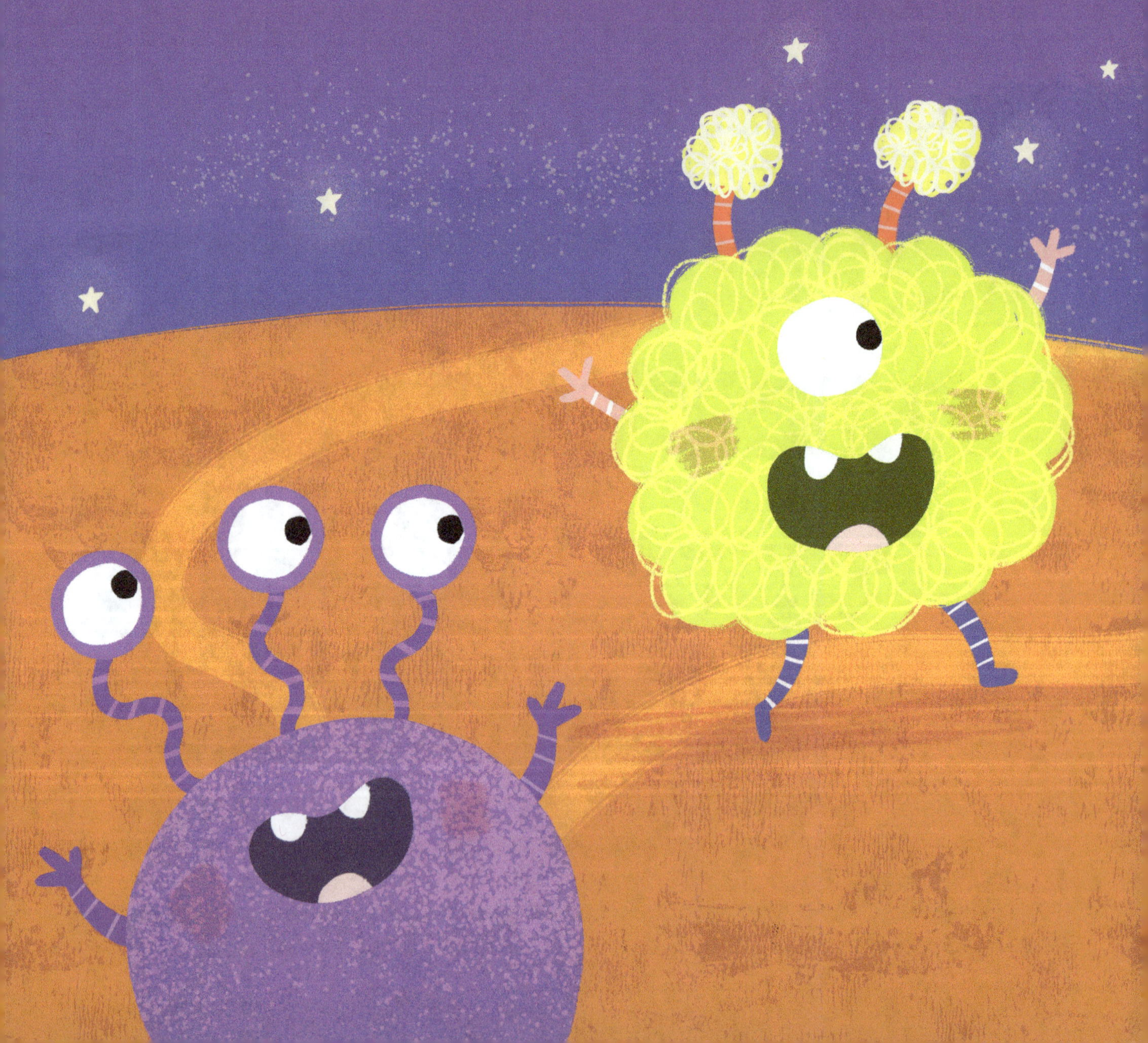

"Doris! We're so glad you're back.
You brought a friend?"

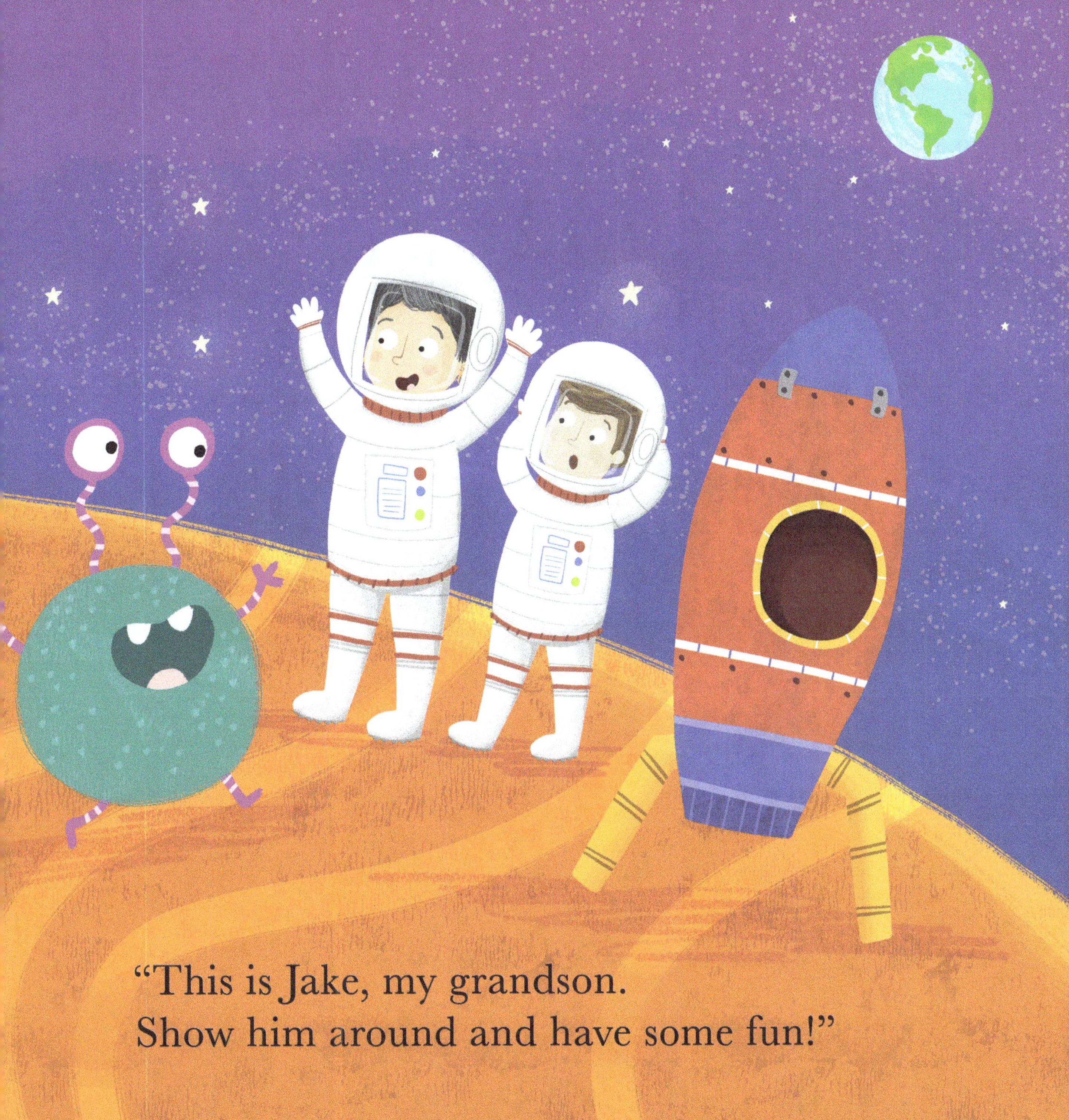

"This is Jake, my grandson.
Show him around and have some fun!"

We play all day.

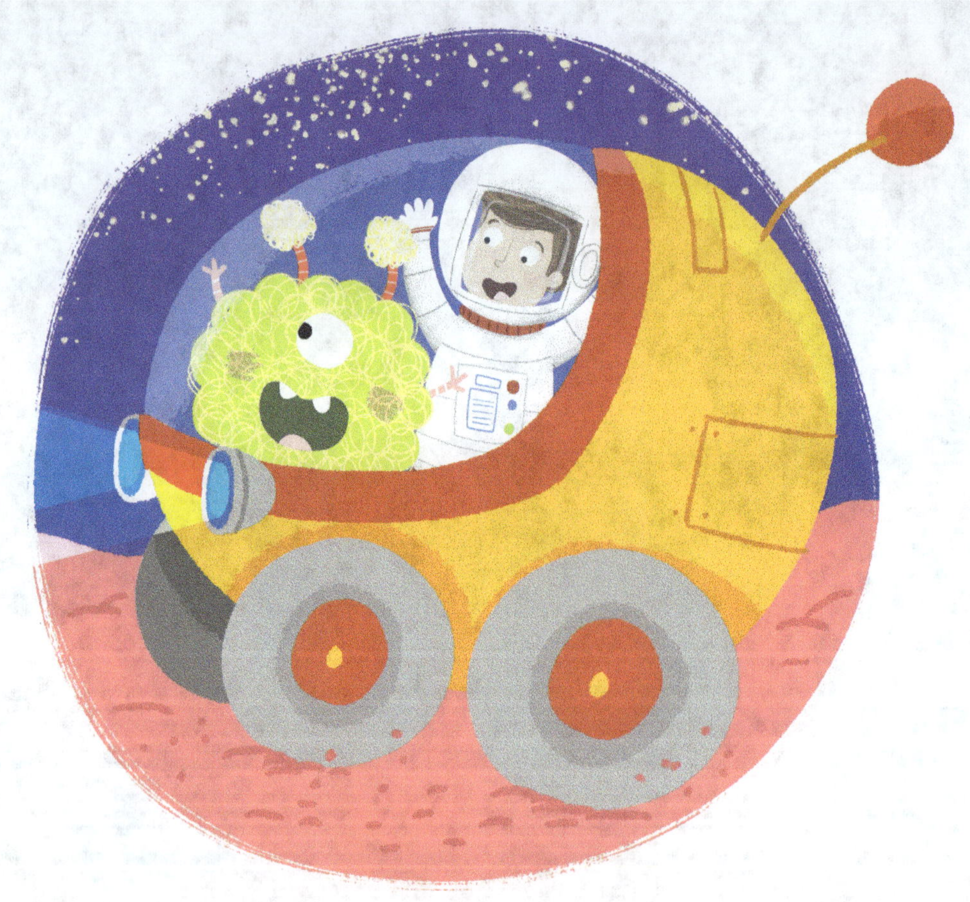

We race the rovers,

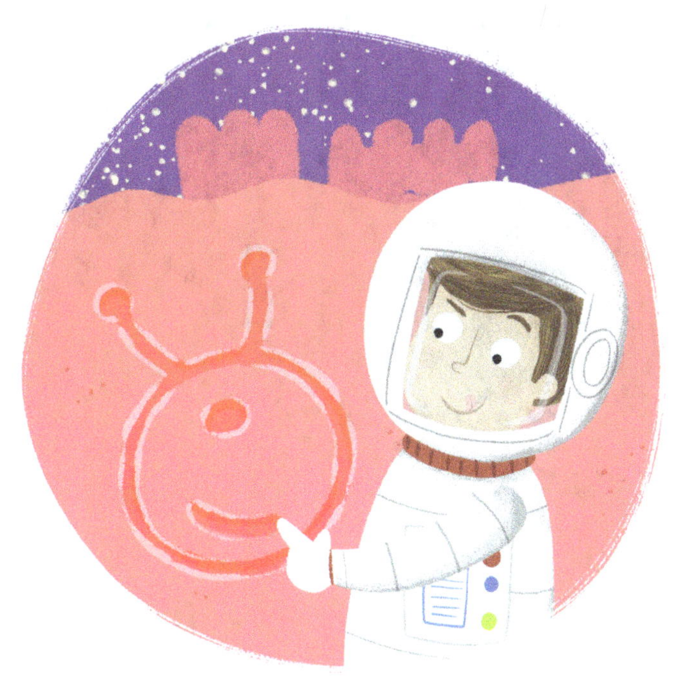

draw on the sand,

and even play pirates.

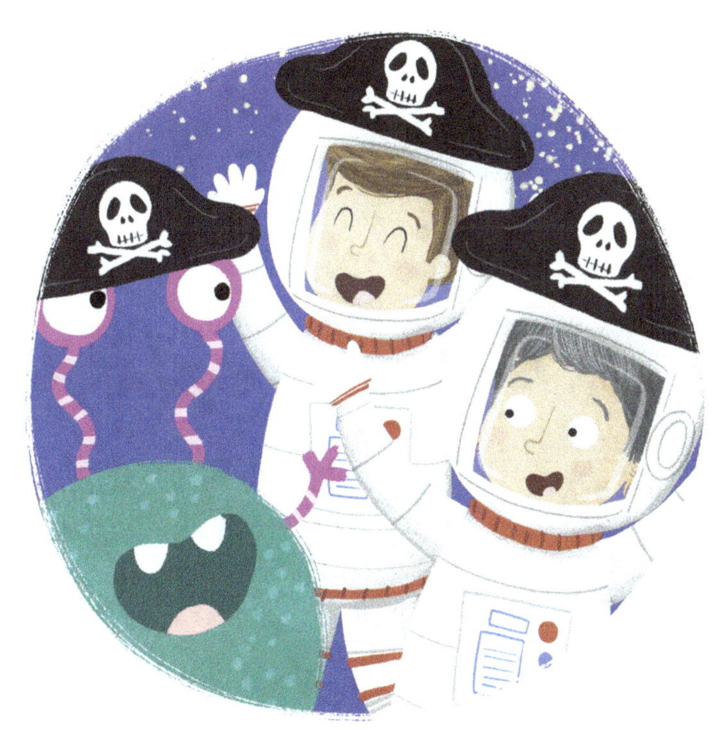

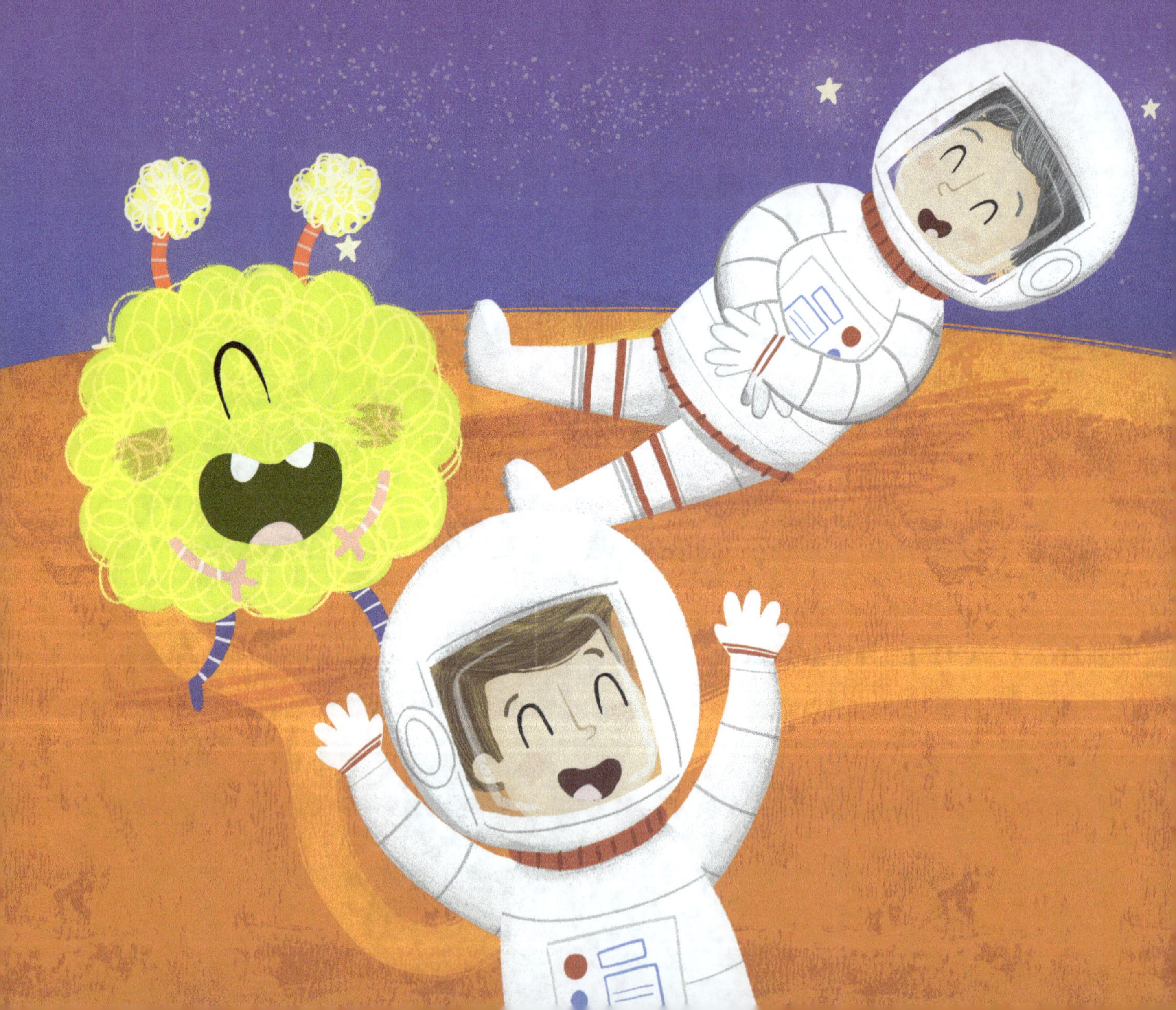
You could probably hear us laughing across
the Milky Way.

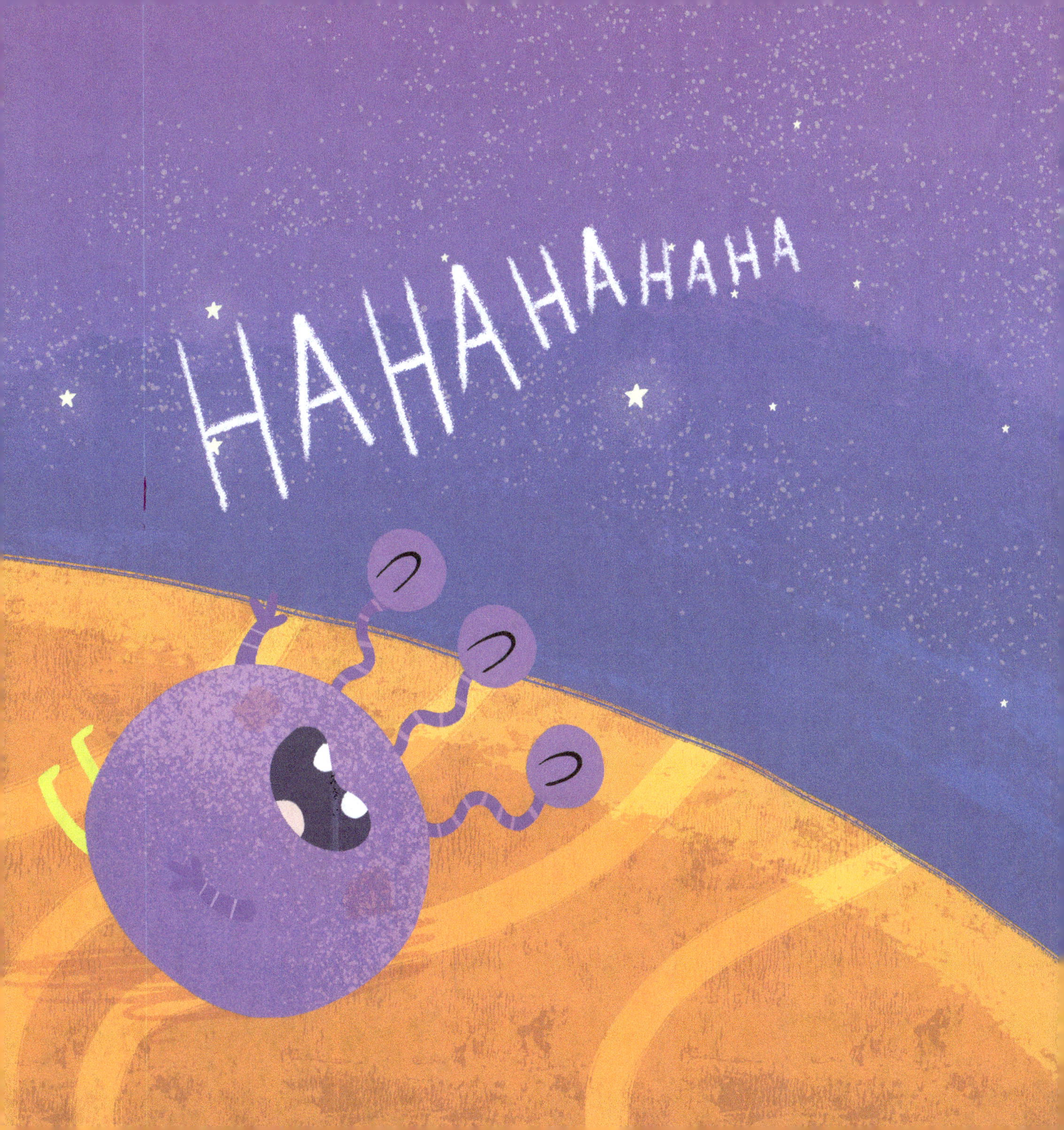

HAHAHAHAHA

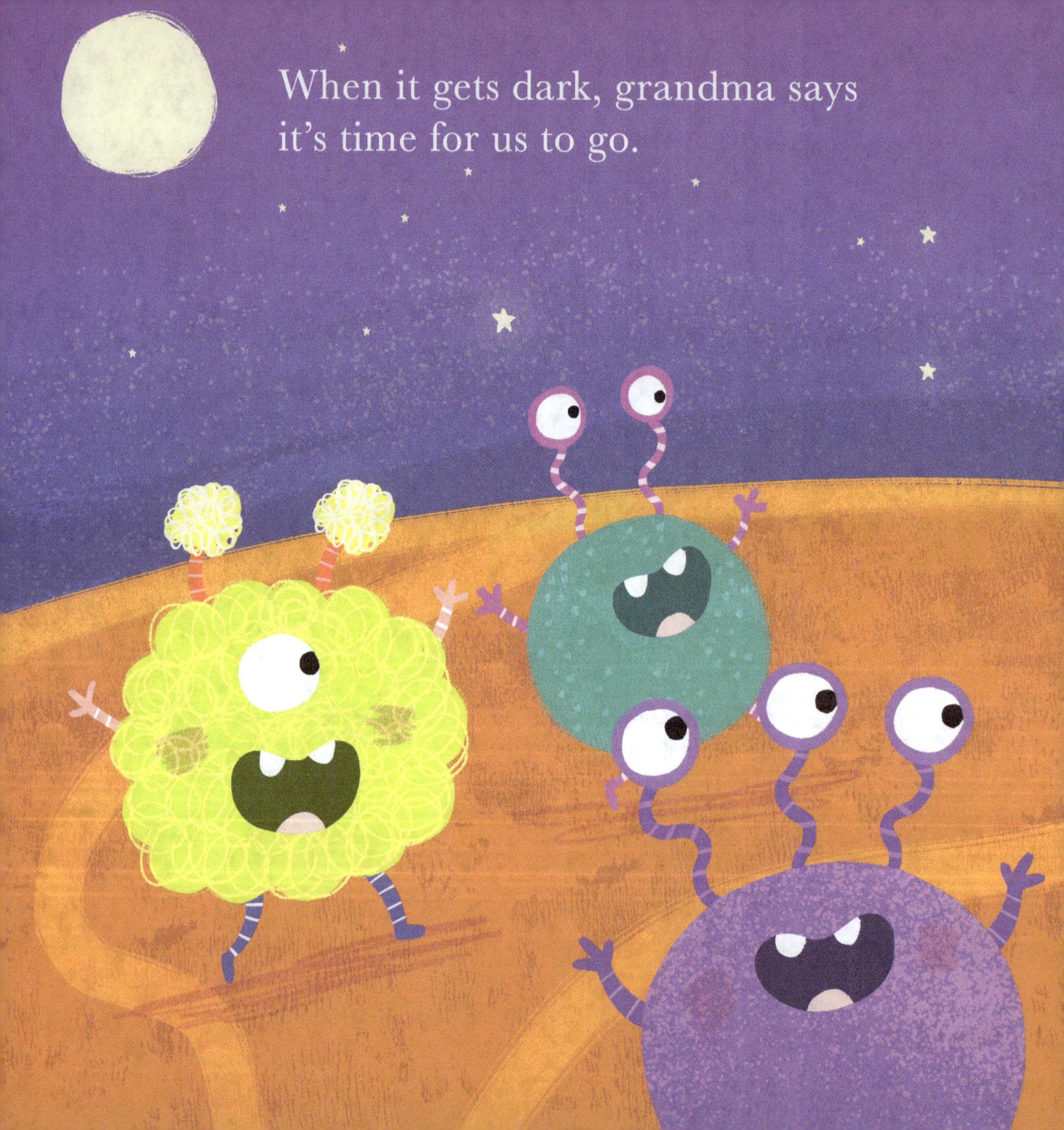
When it gets dark, grandma says
it's time for us to go.

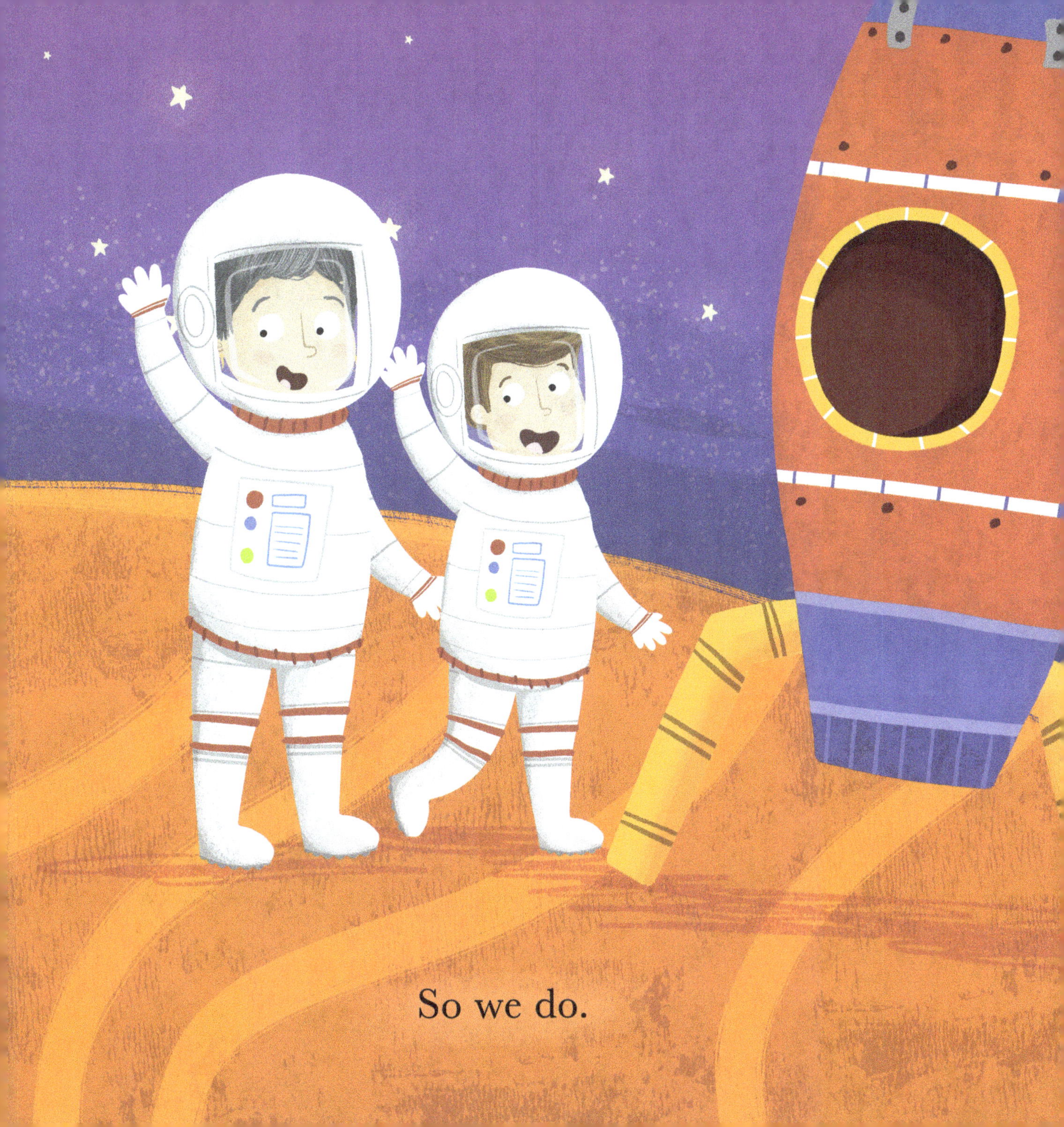

So we do.

I think about my new friends. I wonder if they're thinking about me.

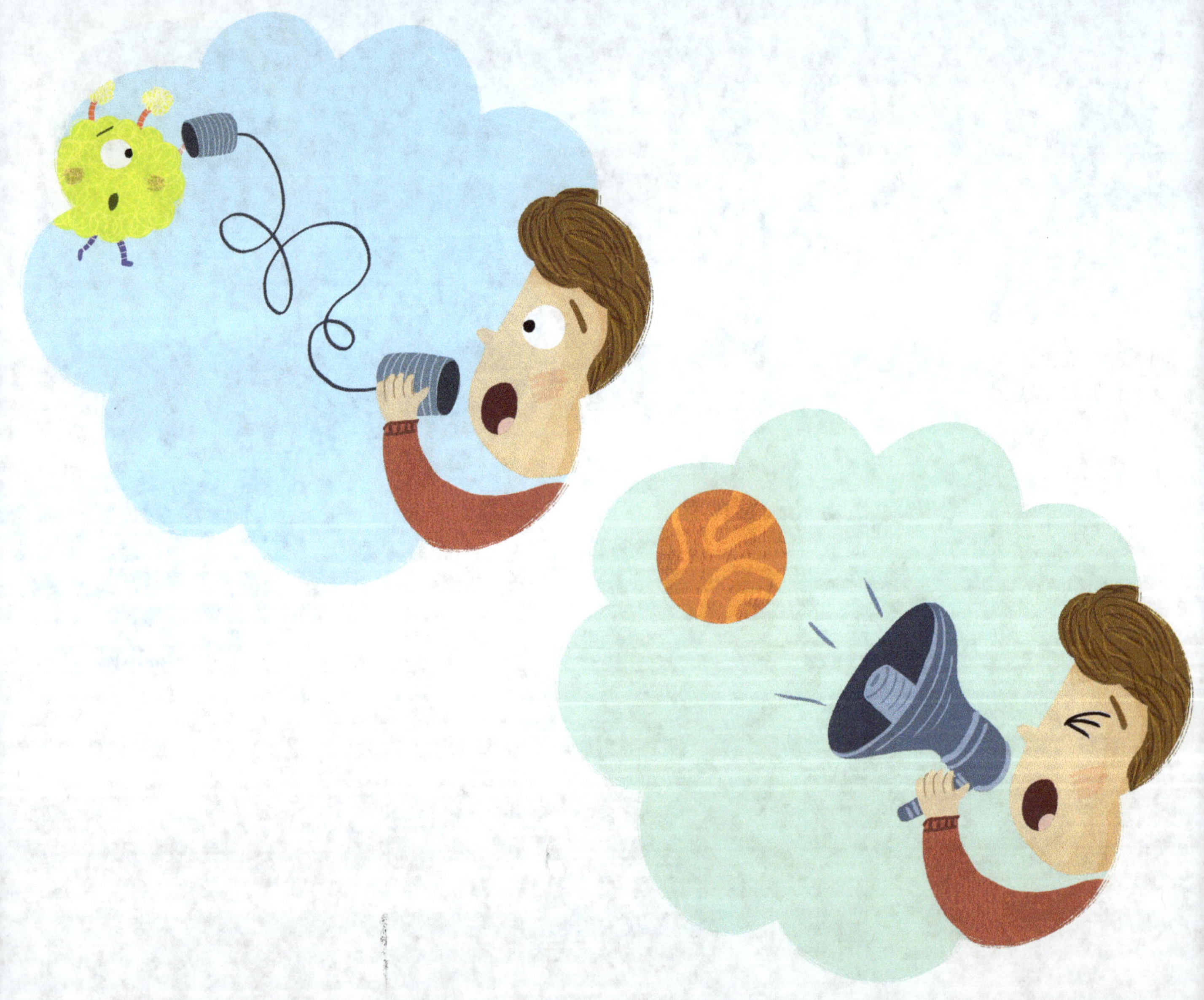

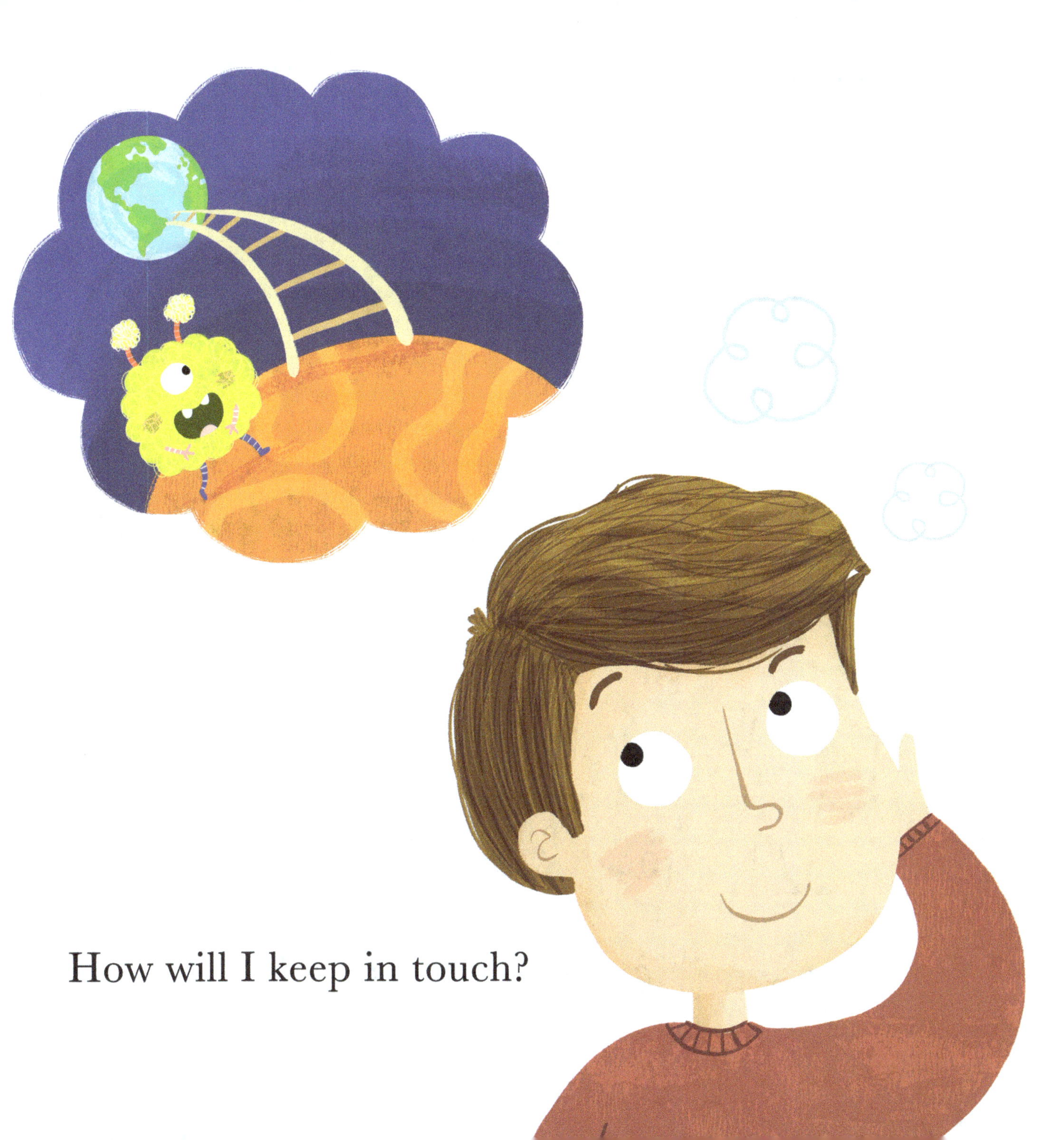

How will I keep in touch?

So now I write letters, too.
I usually get a letter back.

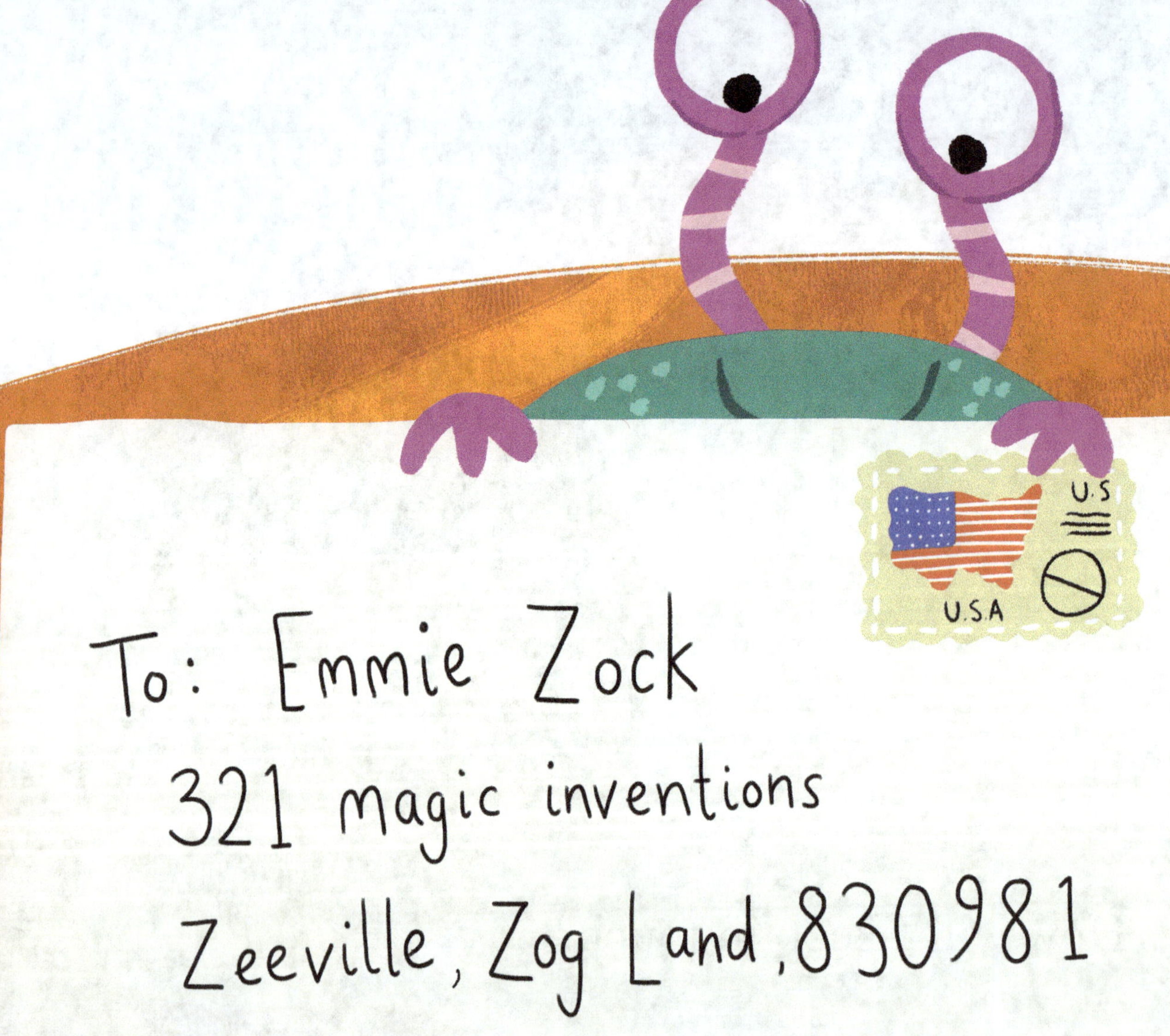

Dear Emmie,
I had so much fun with you!
Look what I made for
us... a pirate ship!

From
Jake

And when I'm not sure which words to say,
I'm glad that grandma is never far away.

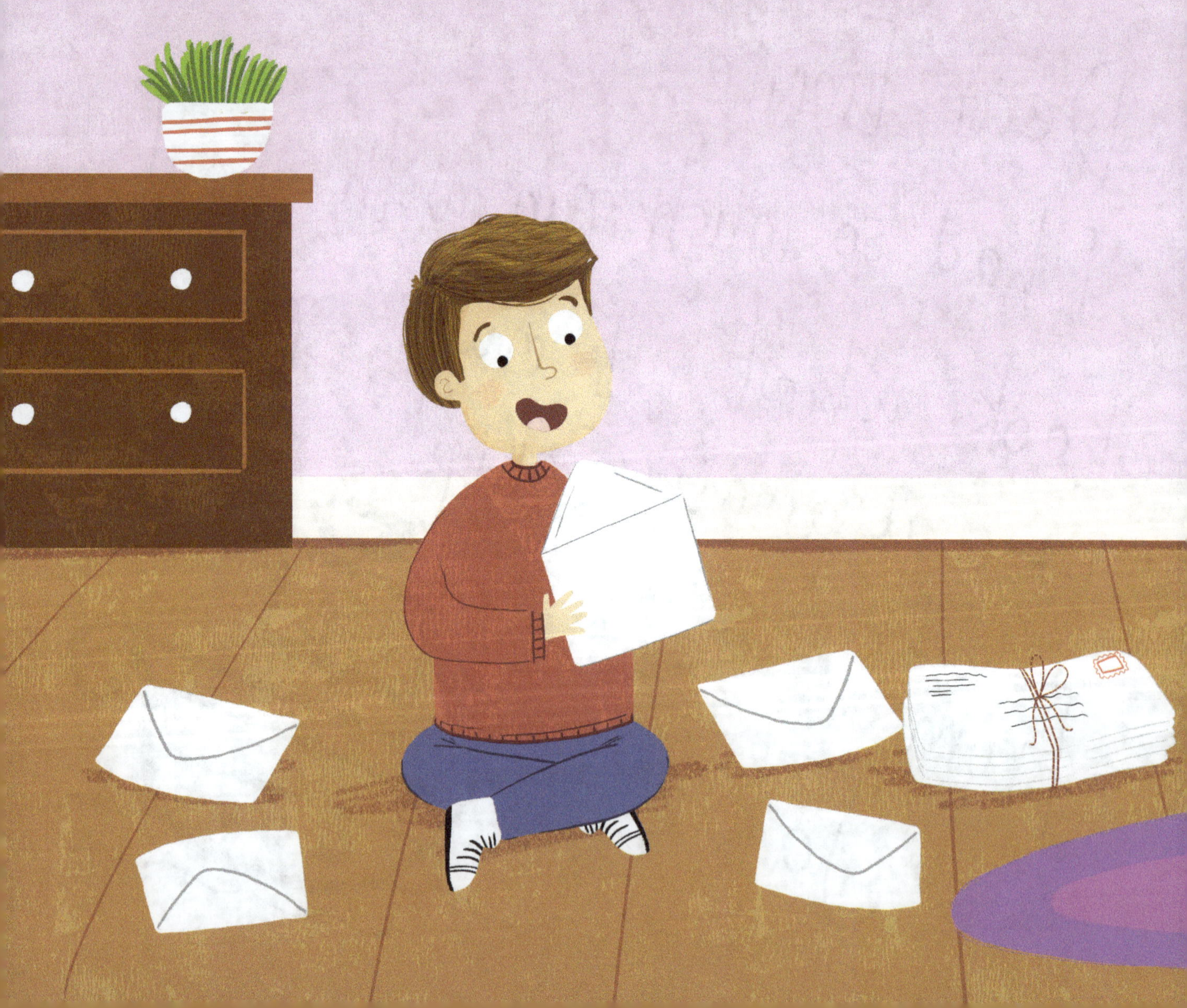

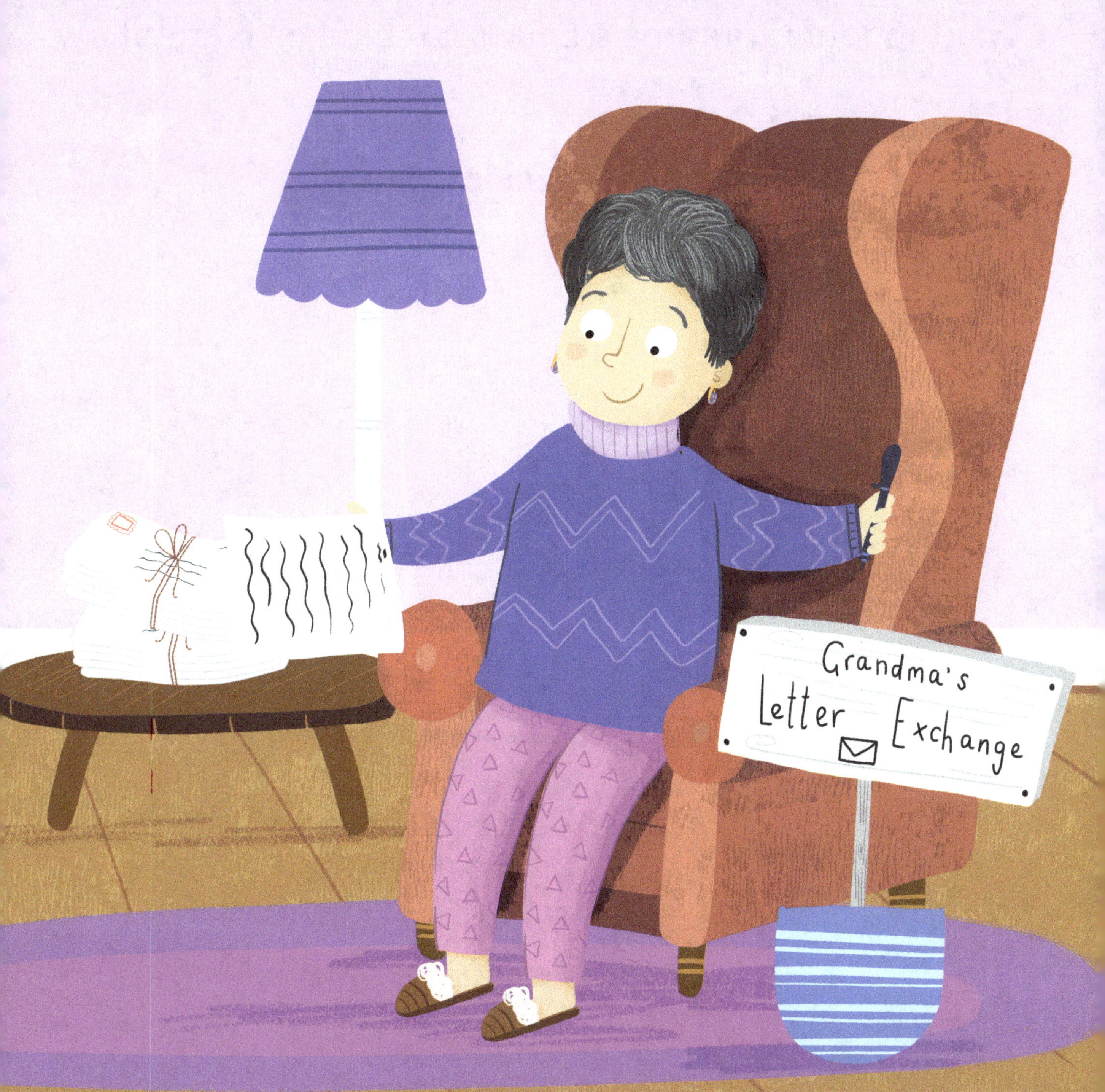
Grandma's
Letter Exchange

Want to join Grandma's Letter Exchange? Here's how:

1. Grab a piece of paper

2. Fold it in half

3.

Write "Dear" and the name of a friend

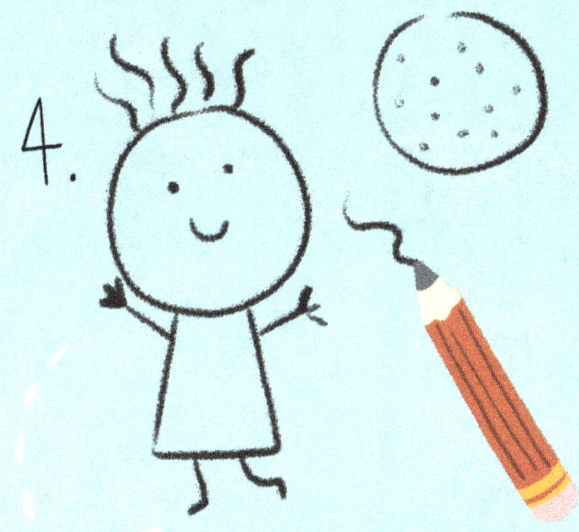

Talk about your favorite things,
tell a joke, or draw a picture.
Then, sign your name.

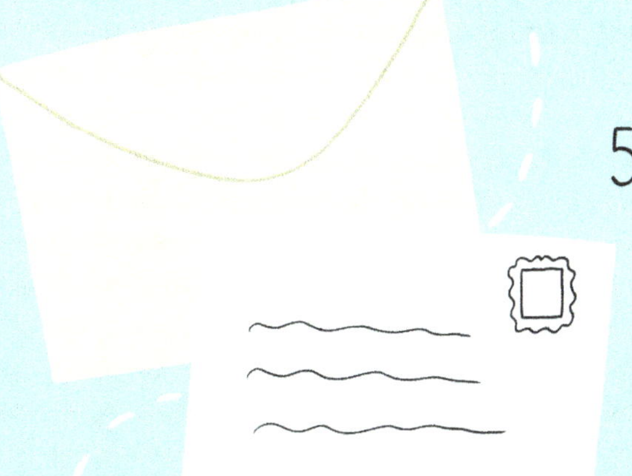

5.

Seal your envelope, and ask
an adult to help you mail it